THE TERMINOLOGY OF THE VEDAS AND EUROPEAN SCHOLARS

THE TERMINOLOGY OF THE VEDAS AND EUROPEAN SCHOLARS

GURU DATTA VIDYARTHI

GYAN

Published by

GYAN

Gyan Publishing House
5, Ansari Road
Daryaganj, New Delhi-110002
Phone: 011-47034999, 9811692060
E-mail: books@gyanbooks.com

Distribution Network
gyanbooks.com
India, USA, Canada, UK, Australia

ISBN: 978-93-6780-712-5 (PB)

First Published, 1893

2nd Impression 2024

Printed at: Gyan Press, Delhi.

THE TERMINOLOGY OF THE VEDAS AND EUROPEAN SCHOLARS
Author: GURU DATTA VIDYARTHI

THE

TERMINOLOGY OF THE VEDAS

AND

EUROPEAN SCHOLARS:

BY

PANDIT GURU DATTA VIDYARTHI, M.A.,
Professor, Physical Science, Government College, Lahore.

CHICAGO EDITION.

Printed and published under the auspices of the
Arya Pratinidhi Sabha, Punjab.

Lahore:
PRINTED AT THE MUFID-I-AM PRESS.

1893.

THE TERMINOLOGY OF THE VEDAS*

AND

EUROPEAN SCHOLARS.

With us, the question of the terminology of the Vedas is of the highest importance, for upon its decision will depend the verdict to be passed by the future world respecting the great controversy to rage between the East and the West, concerning the supremacy of the Vedic philosophy. And even now, the determination of this question involves issues of great value. For, if the Vedic philosophy be true, the interpretations of the Vedas, as given at present by Professor Max Müller and other European scholars must not only be regarded as imperfect, defective and incomplete, but as altogether false. Nay, in the light of true reason and sound scholarship, we are forced to admit their entire ignorance of the very rudiments of Vedic language and philosophy. We are not alone in the opinion we hold. Says Schopenhauer, "I add to this the impression, which the translations of Sanskrit works by European scholars, with very few exceptions, produce on my mind. I cannot resist a certain suspicion that our Sanskrit scholars do not understand their text much better than the higher class of school boys their Greek or Latin." It will be well to note here the opinion of Swami Dayanand Saraswati, the most profound scholar of Sanskrit of his age, on the subject. He says, "The impression that the Germans are the best Sanskrit scholars, and that no one has read so much of Sanskrit as Professor Max Müller, is altogether unfounded. Yes, in a land where lofty trees never grow, even *ricinus communis* or the

* A paper of this name was submitted to the public by the writer early in 1888 but it was necessarily brief and incomplete. It has now been thought advisable to give to the same thoughts and principles a new garb, more suited to the requirements of the reading public of the present day, to amplify the same truths by interesting illustrations, and to supplement them by others that are necessary to complete the treatment of the subject.

castor-oil plant may be called an oak. The study of Sanskrit being altogether out of question in Europe, the Germans and Professor Max Müller may there have come to be regarded as highest authorities.... I came to learn from a letter of a principal of some German University, that even men learned enough to interpret a Sanskrit letter are rare in Germany. I have also made it plain from the study of Max Müller's "History of Sanskrit Literature" and his comments on some *mantras* of the Veda, that Professor Max Müller has been able only to scribble out something by the help of the so-called *tikas*, or paraphrases of the Vedas, current in India."*

It is this want of Vedic scholarship among European scholars, this utter ignorance of Vedic language and philosophy that is the cause of so much misimpression and prejudice even in our own country. We are, indeed, so often authoritatively told by our fellow-brethren who have received the highest English education, but are themselves entirely ignorant of Sanskrit, that the Vedas are books that teach idol-worship or element worship, that they contain no philosophical, moral or scientific truths of any great consequence, unless they be the commonest truisms of the kitchen. It is therefore a matter of greatest concern to learn to attach proper value to the interpretations of these European scholars. We propose, therefore, to present a rough outline of those general principles, according to which Vedic terms should be interpreted, but which European scholars entirely ignore; and hence much of the misinterpretation that has grown up.

In the discussion of philosophical subjects, pre-conceived notions are the worst enemies to encounter. They not only prejudicially bias the mind, but also take away that truthfulness and honest integrity from the soul, which alone are compatible with the righteous pursuit and discernment of TRUTH. In the treatment of a question such as the estimation of the value of system of philosophy or religion, extreme

* Satyartha Prakasha, 3rd Edition, page 278.

sobriety and impartiality of the mind are required. Nor is it to be supposed that a religious or philosophical system can be at once mastered by a mere acquaintance with grammar and language. It is necessary that the mind should, by an adequate previous discipline, be raised to an exalted mental condition, before the recondite and invisible truths of Man and Nature can be comprehended by man. So is it with Vedic philosophy. One must be a complete master of the science of orthœpy, the science of language, the science of etymology, the science of morals, the science of poetry, and the sciences of geology and astronomy;* he must be well versed in the philosophy of *dharma*, the philosophy of characteristics, the doctrines of logic or the science of evidence, the philosophy of essential existences, the philosophy of *yoga*, and the philosophy of *vedanta*;† he must be a master of all these and much more, before he can lay claims to a rational interpretation of the Vedas.

Such, then, should be our Vedic scholars—thorough adepts in science and philosophy, unprejudiced, impartial judges and seekers after truth. But if impartiality be supplanted by prejudice, science and philosophy by quasi-knowledge and superstition, and integrity by motive, whereas predetermination takes the place of honest inquiry, Truth is either disguised or altogether suppressed.

Speaking of the religion of the *Upanishats* and the Bible, says Schopenhauer, who has 'washed himself clean of all early-engrafted Jewish superstitions, and of all philosophy that cringes before these superstitions':—

"In India, our religion (Bible) will now and never strike root; the primitive wisdom of the human race will never be pushed aside by the events of Galilee.‡ On the contrary, Indian wisdom will flow

* These are the well-known six Vedangas:—1. Shiksha, 2. Vyakarana, 3. Nirukta, 4. Kalpa. 5. Chhanda, and 6. Jyotisha.

† These are the well-known six Upangas or Darshanas:—1. Purva Mimansa, 2. Vaisheshika, 3. Nyaya, 4. Sankhya, 5. Yoga, and 6. Vedanta.

‡ It is well-known how the astronomical and geographical discoveries of Galilio and his telescope were forced upon the world in spite of the prisons and death-racks of the so-called Christians.

back upon Europe, and produce a thorough change in our knowing and thinking."

Let us now hear what Professor Max Müller has to say against the remarks of this unprejudiced, impartial philosopher. He says: "Here again, the great philosopher seems to me to have allowed himself to be carried away too far by his enthusiasm for the less known. He is blind for the *dark side of the Upanishat*; and he wilfully shuts his eyes against the bright rays of eternal truths in the Gospel, which even Ram Mohan Roy was quick enough to perceive, behind the mist and clouds of tradition that gather so quickly round the sunrise of every religion."

With the view that the Christianity of Max Müller may be set forth more clearly before the reader, we will quote from the "History of Ancient Sanskrit Literature." Says Max Müller—

"But if India has no place in the political history of the world, it certainly has a right to claim its place in the intellectual history of mankind. The less the Indian nation has taken part in the political struggles of the world, and expended its energies in the exploits of war and the formation of empire, the more it has fitted itself and concentrated all its powers for the fulfillment of the important mission reserved to it in the history of the East. History seems to teach that the whole human race required a gradual education before, in the fulness of time, it could be admitted to the truths of Christianity. All the fallacies of human reason had to be exhausted, before the light of a higher truth could meet with ready acceptance. The ancient religions of the world were but the milk of nature, which was in due time to be succeeded by the bread of life. After the primeval physiolatry, which was common to all members of the Aryan family, had, in the hands of a wily priesthood, been changed into an empty idolatry, the Indian alone, of all the Aryan nations, produced a new form of religion, which has well been called subjective, as opposed to the more objective worship of nature. That religion, the religion of Buddha, has spread far beyond the limits of the Aryan world, and to our limited vision, it may seem to have retarded the advent of Christianity among a large portion of the human race. But in the sight of Him, with whom a thousand years are but as one day, that religion, like all the ancient religions of the world, may have but served to prepare the way of Christ, by helping through its very errors, to strengthen and to deepen the ineradicable yearning of the human heart after the truth of God."*

* Max Müller's History of Ancient Sanskrit Literature, pp. 31—32.

Is not this Christian prejudice? Nór is this with Max Müller alone. Even more strongly does this remark hold good of Monier Williams, whose very object in writing the book, known as "Indian Wisdom," is to caricature the Vedic religion which he calls by the name of Brahmanism, and to hoist up Christianity by the meritorious process of deliberate contrasts. Writes Monier Williams, "It is one of the aims, then, of the following pages to indicate the points of contact between Christianity and the three chief *false religions* of the world, as they are thus represented in India." *

Speaking of Christianity and its claims 'as supernaturally communicated by the common Father of mankind for the good of all His creatures,' he says :—

"Christianity asserts that it effects its aim through nothing short of an entire change of the whole man, and a complete renovation of his nature. The means by which this renovation is effected may be described as a kind of *mutual transfer* or *substitution*, leading to a reciprocal interchange and co-operation between God and man's nature acting upon each other. Man—the Bible affirms—was created in the image of God, but his nature became corrupt through a taint, derived from the fall of the first representative man and parent of the human race, which taint could only be removed by a vicarious death.

"Hence, the second representative man—Christ—whose nature was divine and taintless, voluntarily underwent a sinner's death, that the taint of the old corrupted nature transferred to him might die also. But this is not all. The great central truth of our religion lies not so much in the fact of Christ's death as in the fact of His *continued life*. (Rom. viii. 34). The first fact is that He of His own free-will died ; but the second and more important fact is that He rose again and lives eternally, that He may bestow life for death and a participation in His own divine nature in place of the taint which He has removed.

"This, then, is the reciprocal exchange which marks Christianity and distinguishes it from all other religions—an exchange between the personal man descended from a corrupt parent, and the personal God made man and becoming our second parent. We are separated from a rotten root, and are grafted into a living one. We part with the corrupt will, depraved moral sense, and perverted judgment inherited from the first Adam, and draw re-creative

* Monier William's Indian Wisdom, Introduction, p. 36.

force—renovated wills, fresh springs of wisdom, righteousness, and knowledge—from the ever-living divine stem of the second Adam, to which, by a simple act of faith, we are united. In this manner is the grand object of Christianity effected. Other religions have their doctrines and precepts of morality, which, if carefully detached from much that is bad and worthless, may even vie with those of Christianity. But Christianity has, besides all these, what other religions have not—a personal God, ever living to supply the free grace or regenerating Spirit by which human nature is re-created and again made Godlike, and through which man, becoming once again 'pure in heart,' and still preserving his own will, self-consciousness, and personality, is fitted to have access to God the Father, and dwell in His presence for ever."*

Again, speaking of Brahmanism, he says—

"As to Brahmanism, we must in fairness allow that according to its more fully developed system, the aim of union with God is held to be effected by faith in an apparently personal good, as well as by works and by knowledge. And here some of the lines of Brahmanical thought seem to intersect those of Christianity. But the apparent personality of the various Hindu gods melts away, on closer scrutiny, into a vague spiritual essence. It is true that God becomes man and interposes for the good of men, causing a seeming combination of the human and divine—and an apparent interchange of action and even loving sympathy between the Creator and His creatures. But can there be any real interaction or co-operation between divine and human personalities when all personal manifestations of the Supreme Being—gods as well as men—ultimately merge in the Oneness of the Infinite, and nothing remains permanently distinct from Him? It must be admitted that most remarkable language is used of Krishna (Vishnu), a supposed form of the Supreme, as the source of all life and energy (see pp. 144-148, and see also pp. 456, 457); but if identified with the One God he can only, according to the Hindu theory, be the source of life in the sense of giving out life to re-absorb it into himself. If, on the other hand, he is held to be only an incarnation or manifestation of the Supreme Being in human form, then by a cardinal dogma of Brahmanism, so far from being a channel of life, his own life must be derived from a higher source into which it must finally be merged, while his claim to divinity can only be due to his possessing less of individuality as distinct from God than inferior creatures."†

And lastly in conclusion, he says—

"It is refreshing to turn from such unsatisfying systems, however interspersed with wise and even sublime sentiments, to the living

* Monier William's Indian Wisdom, Introduction, pp. 40—41.

† Ibid, pp. 44—45.

energizing Christianity of European nations, however lamentably fallen from its true standard, or however disgraced by the inconsistencies and shortcomings of nominal adherents—possessors of its name and form without its power."

"In conclusion, let me note one other point which of itself stamps our religion as the only system adapted to the requirements of the whole human race—the only message of salvation intended by God to be gradually pressed upon the acceptance of all His intelligent creatures."*

It is clear, then, that Professor Monier Williams is labouring under hard Christian prejudices, and cannot be viewed in any way as an unprejudiced, impartial student of the Vedas. No wonder then, if modern sophisticated philology, propped by the entire ignorance of the laws of interpretations of Vedic terms, and fed by the prejudices of Christian superstitions, should raise its head against Vedic philosophy and gain audience among European Christian nations or deluded educated natives of India who possess the high merit of being innocent of any knowledge of Sanskrit language or literature.—

But now to the subject. The first canon for the interpretation of Vedic terms, which is laid down by Yaska, the author of Nirukta, is that the Vedic terms are all *yaugika*.† The fourth section of the first chapter of Nirukta opens with a discussion of this very subject. Yaska, Gargya, Shakatayana and all other Grammarians and Etymologists unanimously maintain that Vedic terms are all *yaugika*. But Yaska and Shakatayana also maintain the *rurhi* ‡ terms are also *yaugika*, *i. e.*, were originally framed from the roots; whereas, Gargya maintains that only *rurhi* terms are not *yaugika*. The section concludes with a refutation of the opinions of Gargya, establishing it as

---

* Monier William's Indian Wisdom, Introduction, p. 45.

† A *yaugika* term is one that has a derivative meaning, that is, one that only signifies the meaning of root together with the modifications affected by the affixes. In fact, the structural elements out of which the word is compounded, afford the whole and the only clue to the true signification of the word. The word is purely connotative.

‡ A *rurhi* term is the name of a definite concrete object, where the connotation of the word (as structurally determined) gives no clue to the object denoted by the word. Hence, ordinarily it means a word of arbitrary significance.

true that all terms whether Vedic or *rurhi* are *yaugikas*. It is on this authority of Nirukta that Patanjali quotes in his Mahabhashya the same opinion, and distinguishes the Vedic terms from *Rurhi* terms by the designation of *naigama*. Says Patanjali—

"नाम च धातुजमाह निरुक्ते व्याकरणे शकटस्य च तोकम्"

and a line before this,—

"नैगम रूढिभवं हि सुसाधु" *

The sense of all this is, that all the *Rishis* and *Munis*, ancient authors and commentators without exception, regard Vedic terms to be *yaugika*, whereas *laukika* terms are regarded by some as *rurhi* also.

This principle, the European scholars have entirely ignored, and hence have flooded their interpretations of the Vedas with forged or borrowed tales of mythology, with stories and anecdotes of historic or pre-historic personages. Thus, according to Dr. Muir,† the following historical personages are mentioned in the Rig Veda, the rishis Kanvas, in i, 47-2; Gotamas, in i, 71-16; Gritsamadas, in ii, 39-8; Bhrigavas, in iv, 16-23; and Vrihaduktha, in x, 54-6. But what is the truth! The words Kanva, and Gritsa only signify learned men in general (see Nighantu iii, 13); the word Bhrigavah only signifies men of intellect (see Nighantu, v. 5). The word Gotama signifies one who praises; and Vrihaduktha is simply one whose *ukthas*, or knowledge of natural properties of objects is *vrihat* or complete. It is clear, then, that if this principle is once ignored, one is easily landed into anecdotes of historical or pre-historic personages. The same might be said of Max Müller discovering the story of *Shunah-shepa* in the Rig Veda.. Shepa, which means contact, (Nirukta iii, 2,—(शेपः शपते स्पृशति कर्म्मणो) being suffixed to शुनः or श्वन् which means knowledge (श्वा श्वसतेः शवतेर्वा गतिकर्म्मणः स्यात्) means one who has come into contact with knowledge, *i. e.*, a learned person. It shall appear, in the progress of this article, how *mantra* after *mantra* is misinterpreted by simply falsifying this law of *Nirukta*.

---

* Mahabhashya, Chap. III, Sect. iii, Aph.

† Muir's Sanskrit Texts, Vol. III, pp. 232—234.

To an unprejudiced mind, the correctness of this law will never be doubtful. For, independently of the authority of *Nirukta*, the very antiquity of the Vedas is a clear proof of its words being *yaugika*. And even Professor Max Müller, in his mythological moods, is compelled to confess at least concerning certain positions of the Vedas, that their words are *yaugika*. Says he, " But there is a charm in these primitive strains discoverable in no other class of poetry. Every word retains something of its radical meaning every epithet tells ; every thought, in spite of the most intricate and abrupt expressions, is, if we once disentangle it, true, correct, and complete."*

Further again, says Max Müller, " Names...are to be found in the Veda, as it were, in a still fluid state. They never appear as *appellations* nor yet as *proper names* ; they are organic, not yet broken or smoothed down."†

Can there be anything clearer than this ? The terms occurring in the Vedas are *yaugika*, because "they never appear as appellatives, nor yet as proper names," and because " every word retains something of its radical meaning." It is strange to find that the self-same Max Müller who has perceived the *yaugika* character of words in some *mantras* of the Vedas, should deny the same characteristic to other portions of the Vedas. Having said that words are *yaugika* in these primitive strains, the Vedas, he proceeds to say, "But this is not the case with all the poems of the Veda. It would be tedious to translate many specimens of what I consider the poetry of the secondary age, the Mantra period. These songs are generally intended for sacrificial purposes, they are loaded with technicalities, their imagery is sometimes more brilliant, but always less perspicuous, and many thoughts and expressions are clearly borrowed from earlier hymns."‡ This he calls the *Mantra* period. The primitive strains belong to what is called the

* Max Müller's History of Ancient Sanskrit Literature, page 553.
† Ibid, p. 755.
‡ Ibid, p. 558.

Chhandas period. He describes the characteristics of the *Chhandas* period, as distinguished from the *Mantra* period, that has been above described thus : " There is no very deep wisdom in their teaching, their laws are simple, their poetry shows no very high flights of fancy, and their religion might be told in a few words. But what there is of their language, poetry and religion, has a charm which no other period of Indian literature possesses ; it is spontaneous, original and truthful."* Professor Max Müller quotes Rig Veda, VII. 77, as a specimen hymn of the *Chhandas* period. Says he, " This hymn, addressed to dawn, is a fair specimen of the original simple poetry of the Veda. It has no reference to any special sacrifice, it contains no technical expressions, it can hardly be called a hymn, in our sense of the word. It is simply a poem expressing, without any efforts, without any display of far-fetched thought or brilliant imagery, the feelings of a man who has watched the approach of the dawn with mingled delight and awe, and who was moved to give utterance to what he felt in measured language." †

From these quotations it will be clear that Professor Max Müller regards different portions of the Vedas belonging to different periods. There are some earlier portions, (according to Max Müller's highly accurate calculations, the very exactness and infallibility of which Goldstucker bears ample testimony to) which he calls as belonging to the *Chhandas* period. The word *Chhanda*, in *laukika* Sanskrit, means spontaneity. Hence he regards *Chhandas* period to be the one, the hymns of which period only teach common things, are free from the flight of fancy, and are the spontaneous utterances of a simple (foolish) mind. The *Mantra* period (2,900 years older) is full of technicalities and descriptions of elaborate ceremonies. Now we ask what proof has Max Müller given to prove that the different portions of the Vedas belong to different periods. His proofs are only two. Firstly, the ill-conceived, confused idea of the difference between *Chhandas* and

---

* Max Müller's History of Ancient Sanskrit Literature, p. 526.

† Ibid, p. 552.

Mantras; and secondly, the different phases of thought represented by the two portions.

We will consider each of these reasons in details.

Says Yaska—

मन्त्रः मननात् छन्दांसि छादनात् स्तोमः स्तवनात्
यजुर्यजतेः सामसंमितमृचा ॥ निरु० ७ । १२ ॥

which means that there is no difference in the meaning of *mantra* and *chhandas*. The Veda is called the *mantra*, as through it one learns the true knowledge of all existences. The Veda is also called the *chhandas*, as it removes all ignorance, and brings one under the protection of true knowledge and happiness. Or, more explicitly still, we read in *Shatapatha*, VIII. 2.—

छन्दांसि वै देवा वयोनाधाश्छन्दोभिर्हीदं सर्वं वयुनं नद्धं ॥

The *mantras* (*deva*) are called *chhandas* for a knowledge of all human conduct is bound up with them. It is through them that we learn all righteous conduct. The *yaugika* sense of the words will also lead to the same conclusion. *Mantra* may be derived from the root *man*, to think, or *matri*, to reveal the secret knowledge. Panini thus derives the word *chhandas* : चन्देरादेश्छः ॥* *Chhandas* is derived from the root *chadi* to delight or illumine. *Chhandas* is that the knowledge of which produces all delight or which illumines every thing, *i.e.*, reveals its true nature.

The second reason of Max Müller for assigning different periods to different portions of the Vedas, is that there are two different phases of thought discoverable in the Vedas. The one is the truthful and simple phase of thought and corresponds to his *Chhandas* period. The other is the elaborate and technical phase of thought that corresponds to his *Mantra* period. But what proof has Max Müller to show that the hymns of his secondary period are full of

---

* Unadi Kosha, iv. 219.

elaborate and technical thought? Evidently this, that he interprets them thus. If his interpretations were proved to be wrong, his distinction of the two periods will also fall to the ground. Now, why does he interpret the hymns of the *mantra* period thus? Evidently, because on the anthority of Sayana and Mahidhara, he takes the words of those *mantras* to signify technicalities, sacrifices, and artificial objects and ceremonies, or, in other words, he takes these words not in their *yaugika,* but in their *rurhi* sense. It is clear, then, that if Max Müller had kept in view the canon of interpretation given in Nirukta, that all Vedic words are *yaugika,* he would not have fallen into the fallacious anachronism of assigning different periods to different parts of the Vedas.

But there is another prejudice which is cherished by many scholars evidently under the impression of its being a well-recognised scientific doctrine. It is that in the ruder stages of civilization when laws of nature are little known and but very little understood, when mankind has not enough of the experience of the world, strict methods of correct reasoning are very seldom observed. On the other hand, analogy plays a most important part in the performance of intellectual functions of man.

The slightest semblance, or visage of semblance, is enough to justify the exercise of analogy. The most palpable of the forces of nature impress the human mind in such a period of rude beginnings of human experience by motions mainly. The wind blowing, the fire burning, a stone falling, or a fruit dropping, affects the senses essentially as moving. Now, throughout the range of conscious exertion of muscular power *will* precedes motion, and, since even the most grotesque experience of a savage in this world assumes this knowledge, it is no great stretch of intellectual power to argue that these natural forces also, to which the sensible motions are due, are endowed with the faculty of will. The personification of the forces of nature being thus effected, their deification soon follows. The overwhelming potency, the unobstructible might, and often the violence, with which, in the sight of a savage, these forces operate, strike him with terror, awe and reverence. A sense of his own weakness, humility and inferiority creeps over the savage mind, and, what was intellectually personified, becomes emotionally deified. According to this view, the Vedas, undoubtedly books of primitive times, consist of prayers from such an emotional character addressed to the forces of nature including wind and rain—prayers breathing passions of the savage for vengeance or for propitiation or in moments of poetic exaltation, hymns simply portraying the simple phenomena of nature in the personified language of mythology.

It is therefore more agreeable for these scholars to believe that the Vedas, no doubt books of primitive times, are records of the mythological lore of the ancient Aryans.

And since, even according to the confessions of Max Müller, higher truths of philosophy and monotheism are to be found here and there in the Vedas, it has become difficult to reconcile the mythological interpretations of the main part of the Vedas with the philosophical portions. Says Max Müller, "I add only one more hymn [Rig. x. 121] in which the idea of one God is expressed with such power and decision that it will make us hesitate before we deny to the Aryan nations an instinctive monotheism."* It is therefore argued by some that the mythological portions are earlier than philosophical ones; for the primitive faith as already indicated is always mythology.

The fundamental error of this supposition lies in regarding a contingent conclusion as a necessary one; for although mythology may be the result of barbarous intellect and analogical reasoning, it is not necessarily always so. It may even grow up as a degenerate, deformed and petrified remnant of a purer and truer religion. The history of

---

* Max Müller's History of Ancient Sanskrit Literature, p. 568.

religious practices, primarily designed to meet certain real wants, degenerating, after a lapse of time, on the cessation of those wants, into mere ceremonies and customs, is an ample testimony of the truth of the above remarks. Had the European scholars never come across the mythological commentaries of Sayana and Mahidhara, or the *puranic* literature of post-vedic, (nay anti-vedic) period, it would have been impossible for them, from the mere grounds of comparative mythology or Sanskrit philosophy, to alight on such interpretations of the Vedas as are at present current among them. May it not be, that the whole mythological fabric of the *puranas,* later as they are, was raised long after the vitality of true Vedic philosophy had departed from their words in the sight of the ignorant pedants ? Indeed, when one considers that the *Upanishats* inculcate that philosophical monotheism, the parallel of which does not exist in the world—a monotheism, that can only be conceived after a full conviction in the uniformity of nature,—and that they together with the philosophical *darshanas* all preceded the *puranas ;* when one considers all this, one can hardly resist the conclusion that, at least in India, mythology rose as a rotten remnant of the old philosophical living religion of the Vedas. When through the ignorance of men, the *yaugika* meanings of the Vedic words were forgotten, and proper names interpreted instead, there grew up a morbid mythology, the curse of modern idolatrous India. That mythology may thus arise on account of the decay of the primitive meaning of old words, even Professor Max Müller admits, when speaking of the degeneration of truth into mythology by a process, he styles '*dialectic growth and decay*' or dialectic life of religion. He says—

" It is well known that ancient languages are particularly rich in synonyms, or, to speak more correctly, that in them the same object is called by many names—is, in fact, polynymous. While in modern languages most objects have one name only, we find in ancient Sanskrit, in ancient Greek and Arabic, a large choice of words for the same subject. This is perfectly natural. Each name could express one side only of whatever had to be named, and not satisfied with one partial name, the early framers of language produced one name after the other, and after a time retained those which seemed most useful for special purposes. Thus the sky might be called not only the brilliant, but the dark, the covering, the thundering, the rain-giving. This is the polyonomy of language, and it is what we are accustomed to call polytheism in religion.* &c. &c. (pp. 276-277.)

Even, in the face of these facts, European scholars are so very reluctant to leave their pre-conceived notions that, as an example of the same influence, Frederick Pincott writes to me from England:

"You are right in saying that the commentators, now so much admired, had very little, if any, better means of knowledge on Vedic Terminology than we have at present. And you are certainly right in treating the Puranas as very modern productions; but you are wrong in deducing India's mythological notions from such recent works. The Rig Veda itself, undoubtedly the oldest book which India possesses, abounds in mythological matter."

Do the expressions "you are certainly right," and "you are wrong" amount to any proof of the Vedas abounding in mythology? But further he says, "After the great shock which the spread of Buddhism gave to the old Indian form of faith, the Brahmans began to make their faith seriously philosophical in the *Darshanas*. Of course, many bold philosophical speculations are found in the *Upanishats* and even in the *Sanhitas*; but it was at the time of the *Darshanas* that the religion was placed on a really philosophical basis."

Nothing shows so great a disrespect towards the history of another nation as the above. One is indeed wonder-struck at the way in which European scholars mistrust Indian chronology, and force their hypothetical guess-work and conjecture before the world as a sound historical statement of facts. Who, that has impartially studied the *darshana* literature, does not know that the *darshanas* existed centuries before even the first word of Buddhism was uttered in India? Jaimini, Vyasa and Patanjali had gone by, Gautama, Kanada and Kapila were buried in the folds of oblivion when Buddhism sprang up in the darkness of ignorance. Even the great Shankara, who waged a manly war against Buddhism or Jainism, preached nearly 2,200 years

* Max Müller's Lectures on the Science of Religion, pp. 276-277.

ago. Now this Shankara is a commentator on Vyasa Sutras, and was preceded by Gaudapâda and other Achâryas in his work. Generations upon generations had passed away after the time of Vyasa when Shankara was born. Further, there is no event so certain in Indian History as Mahâbhârata, which took place about 4,900 years ago. The *darshanas*, therefore, existed at least 4,900 years ago. There is a strong objection against the admission of these facts by European scholars, and that objection is the Bible. For, if these dates be true, what will become of the account of creation as given in the Bible ? It seems, besides, that European scholars, on the whole, are unfit to comprehend that there could be any disinterested literature in the past. It is easier for them to comprehend that political or religious revolutions or controversies should give rise to new literature through necessity. Hence the explanations of Mr. Pincott. The old Brahmans were superstitious, dogmatic believers in the revelations of the Vedas. When Buddhism spread like wild fire, they thought of shielding their religion by mighty arguments and hence produced the *darshana* literature. This assumption so charmingly connects heterogeneous events together that although historically false, it is worth being believed in for the sake of its ingenious explauatory power.

To return to the subject. Yaska lays down a canon for the interpretation of Vedic terms. It is that the Vedic terms are *yaugika*. Mahâbhâshya repeats the same. We have seen how this law is set aside and ignored by the European scholars in the interpretations of the Vedas, whence have arisen serious mistakes in their translations of the Vedas. We have also seen how Dr. Muir falling in the same mistake interprets general terms as proper nouns; and how Max Müller also led by the same error, wrongly divides the Vedas into two parts; the *Chhandas* and *Mantras.* We have also seen how due to the ignorance of the same law, *Mantras* upon *Mantras* have been interpreted as mythological in meaning, whereas some few Mantras could only be interpreted philosophically, thus giving rise to the question of reconciling philosophy with mythology. To further illustrate the importance of the proposition, that all Vedic terms are *yaugika*, I herewith subjoin the true translation of the 4th Mantra of the 50th Sukta of Rig Veda with my comments thereon and the translation of the same by Monier Williams for comparison. Surya, as a *yaugika* word, means both the sun and the Divinity. Monier Williams takes it to represent the sun only. Other terms will become explicit in the course of exposition. The *Mantra* runs as follows :—

तरणिर्विश्वदर्शतो ज्योतिष्कृदसि सूर्य्य । विश्वमा भासि रोचनं ॥

The subject is the gorgeous wonders of the solar and the electric worlds. "A grand problem is here propounded in this *Mantra*. Who is here that is not struck with the multiplicity of objects and appearances ? Who that has not lost thought itself in contemplation of the infinite varieties that inhabit even our own planet ? Even the varieties of plant life have not yet been counted. The number of animal and plant species together with the vast number of mineral compounds may truly be called infinite." But why confine ourselves to this earth alone. Who has counted the host of heavens and the infinity of stars, the innumerable number of worlds yet made, and still remaining to be made? What mortal eye can measure and scan the depths of space ? Light travels at the rate of 180,000 miles per second. There are stars from which rays of light have started on their journey ever since the day of creation, hundreds of years ago, the rays have sped on and on with the unearthly velocity of 180,000 miles per second through space, and have only now penetrated into the atmosphere of our earth. Imagine the infinite depth of space with which we are on all sides surrounded. Are we not struck with variety and diversity in every direction? Is not differentiation the universal formula ? Whence have these manifold and different objects of the universe proceeded ? How is it that the same Universal-Father-spirit permeating in all and acting on all produced these heterogeneous items of the universe ? Where lies the cause of difference ? A difference so striking and at once so beautiful ? How can the same God acting upon the universe produce an earth here and a sun there, a planet here and a satellite there, an ocean here and a dry land there, nay, a Swami here and an idiot there? The answer to this question is impressed in the very solar constitution. Scientific philosophers assure us that colour is not an intrinsic property of matter as popular belief would have it. But it is an accident of matter. A red object appears red not because it is essentially so, but because of an extraneous cause. Red and violet would appear equally black when placed in the dark. It is the magic of sunbeams which imparts to them this special influence, this chromatic beauty, this congenial coloration. In a lonely forest mid gloom and wilderness, a weary traveller who had betaken himself to the alluring shadow of a pompous tree, lay down to rest and there sunk in deep slumber. He awoke and found himself enveloped in gloom and dismal darkness on all sides. No earthly object was visible on either side. A thick black firmament on high, so beclouded as to inspire with the conviction that the sun had never shone there, a heavy gloom on the right, a gloom on the left, a gloom before and a gloom behind. Thus laboured the traveller under the ghastly, frightful windspell of frozen darkness. Immediately the heat-carrying rays of the sun struck upon the massive cloud, and, as if by a magic touch, the frozen gloom began to melt, a heavy shower of rain fell down. It cleared the atmosphere of suspended dust particles; and, in a twinkling of the eye, fled the moisture-laden sheet of darkness resigning its realm to awakened vision entire. The traveller turned his eyes in ecstatic wonder from one direction to the other, and beheld a dirty gutter flowing there, a crystalline pond reposing here, a green grass meadow more beautiful than violet plant on one side, and a cluster of variegated fragrant flowers on the other. The feathery creation with peacock's train, and deer's slender legs, and chirrup of birds with plumage lent from Heaven, all, in fact, all darted into vision. Was there naught before the sun had shone? Had verdant forest, rich with luxuriant vegetation, and filled with the music of birds all grown in a moment? Where lay the crystalline waters? Where the blue canopy, where the fragrant flower? Had they been transported there by some magical power in a twinkling of the eye from dark dim distant region of chaos? No, they did not spring up in a moment. They were already there. But the sunbeams had not shed their lustre on them. It required the magic of the lustrous sun to shine, before scenes of exquisite beauty could dart into vision. It required the luminous rays of the resplendent orb to shed their influence before the eyes could roll in the beautiful, charming, harmonious, reposeful and refreshing scenes of fragrant green. Yes, thus, even thus, is this sublimely attractive Universe, रोचनं विश्वं, illuminated by a sun सूर्यआभासि, the Sun that knows no setting, the Sun that caused our planets and the solar orb to appear ज्योतिष्कृद्, the Sun that evolves the panorama of this grand creation, विश्वदर्शत, the eternal Sun ever existing through eternity in perpetual action for the good of all. *He* sheds the rays of His wisdom all around; the deeply thirsty, and parching, blast-dried atoms of matter drank in, to satiation, from the ever-flowing, ever-gushing, ever-illuminating rays of Divine wisdom, their appropriate elements and essences of phenomenal existence and panoramic display. Thus is this universe sustained. One central sun producing infinity of colours. One central Divinity, producing infinity of worlds and objects. Compare with this Monier William's translation :—

> "With speed beyond the ken of mortals, thou, O sun,
> Dost ever travel on, conspicuous to all.
> Thou dost create the light, and with it illume
> The entire universe."

We have shown why we regard *Chhandas* and *Mantra* as synonymous. We have also seen how Max Müller distinguishes between *Chhandas* and *Mantra*, regarding the latter as belonging to the secondary age, as loaded with technicalities, and as being less perspicuous than the former. He points out its chief character to be that "these songs are generally intended for sacrificial purposes." Concerning this *Mantra* period, he says, "One specimen may suffice, a hymn describing the sacrifice of the horse with the full detail of a superstitious ceremonial. (Rig Veda, i. 162)."

We shall therefore quote the 162nd Sukta of Rigveda, as it is the specimen hymn of Max Müller, with his translation, and show how, due to a defective knowledge of Vedic literature and to the rejection of the principle that Vedic terms are all *yaugika*, Professor Max Müller translates a purely scientific hymn, distinguishable in no characteristics from the *chhandas* of the Vedas, as representative of an *artificial, cumbersome* and *highly superstitious* ritual or ceremonial.

To our thinking, Müller's interpretation is so very incongruous, unintelligible, and superficial, that were the interpretation even regarded as *possible*, it could never be conceived as the description of an *actual* ceremonial. And now to the hymn. The first *mantra* runs thus :—

मानो मित्रो वरुणो अर्यमायुरिन्द्र ऋभुक्षा मरुतः परिख्यन् ।
यद्वाजिनो देवजातस्य सप्तेः प्रवक्ष्यामो विदथे वीर्य्याणि ॥ १ ॥

Max Müller translates it, "May Mitra, Varuna, Aryaman, Ayu, Indra, the lord of the Ribhus, and the Maruts not rebuke us, because we shall proclaim at the sacrifice the virtues of the swift horse sprung from the gods."

That the above interpretation may be regarded as real or as true, let Professor Max Müller prove that Aryans of the Vedic times entertained the superstition that at least one swift horse had sprung from the gods, also that the gods Mitra, Varuna, Aryaman, Ayu, Indra, the lord of Ribhus and the Maruts, did not like to hear the virtues of the swift horse proclaimed at the sacrifice, for, if otherwise, they would have no reason to rebuke the poet. Not one of these positions it is ever possible to entertain with validity. Even the most diseased conception of a savage shrinks from such a superstition as the "swift horse sprung from the gods." It is also in vain to refer for the verification of this position to the *ashwamedha* of the so-called *Puranas.* The whole truth is that this mythology of *ashwamedha* arose in the same way in which originates Max Müller's translation. It originates from an ignorance of the dialectic laws of the Vedas, when words having a *yaugika* sense are taken for proper nouns, and an imaginary mythology started.

To take, for instance, the *mantra* quoted above. Max Müller is evidently under the impression that Mitra is the 'god of the day,' Varuna is the god of the 'investing sky,' Vayu or Ayu is the 'god of the wind,' Indra the 'god of the watery atmosphere,' Ribhus, 'the celestial artists,' and Maruts are the 'storm-gods.' But why these gods? Because he ignores the *yaugika* sense of these words and takes them as propor nouns. Literally speaking, *mitra* means a friend; *varuna,* a man of noble qualities; *aryama,* a judge or an administrator of justice; *ayu,* a learned man; *indra,* a governor; *ribhuksha,* a wise man; *marutahs,* those who practically observe the laws of seasons. The word *ashwa* which occurs in the *mantra* does not mean 'horse' only, but it also means the group of three forces—heat, electrictity and magnetism. It, in fact, means anything that can carry soon through a distance. Hence writes Swami Dayanand in the beginning of this Sukta:—

अथाश्वस्य विद्युद्रूपेण व्याप्तस्याग्नेश्च विद्यामाह ॥

"This Sukta is an exposition of *ashwa vidya* which means the science of training horses and the science of heat which pervades everywhere in the shape of electricity." That '*ashwa*' means heat, will be clear from the following quotations:—

अश्वं न त्वा वारवन्तम् विदध्या अग्निं नमोभिः ॥ Rig Veda.

The words *ashwam agnim* show that *ashwa* means *agni* or Heat. And further—

वृषो अग्निः समिध्यते ऽश्वो न देववाहनः । तं हविष्मन्त ईडते ॥

(Rv. i. 27. I.)

which means: *Agni,* the *ashwa,* carries like an animal of conveyance the learned who thus recognize its distance-carrying properties. Or further—

वृषो अग्निः। अश्वो ह वा एष भूत्वा देवेभ्यो यज्ञं वहति॥

Shatapatha Br. I. iii. 3.29-30.

The above quotations are deemed sufficient to show both meanings of *ashwa* above indicated.

Professor Max Müller translates the "*devajata*" of the *mantra* as "sprung from the gods." This is again wrong, for he again takes *deva* in its popular (*laukika*) sense, god; whereas *devajata* means "with brilliant qualities manifested, or evoked to work by learned men:" the word *deva* meaning both brilliant qualities and learned men. Again Max Müller translates "*virya*" merely into virtues, instead of "power-generating virtues." The true meaning of the *mantra*, therefore, is—

"We will describe the power-generating virtues of the energetic horses endowed with brilliant properties, or the virtues of the vigorous force of heat which learned or scientific men can evoke to work for purposes of appliances (not sacrifice). Let not philanthropes, noble men, judges, learned men, rulers, wise men and practical mechanics ever disregard these properties." With this compare Max Müller's translation—

"May Mitra, Varuna, Aryaman, Ayu, Indra, the lord of Ribhus, and the Maruts not rebuke us, because we shall proclaim at the sacrifice the virtues of the swift horse sprung from the gods."

We come now to the second *mantra* which runs thus:—

यन्निर्णिजारेक्णसा प्रावृतस्य रातिं गृभीतां मुखतो नयन्ति।
सुप्राङजो मेम्यद्विश्वरूप इन्द्रापूष्णोः प्रियमप्येति पाथः॥ २॥

Max Müller translates it thus—

"When they lead before the horse, which is decked with pure gold ornaments, the offering, firmly grasped, the spotted goat bleats while walking onwards; it goes the path beloved by Indra and Púshan."

Here again there is no sense in the passage. The bleating of the goat has no connection with the leading of the offering before the horse, nor any with its walking onward. Nor is the path of Indra and Púshan in any way defined. In fact, it is very clear that there is no definite specific relation between the first *mantra* and this according to Müller's translation, unless a far-fetched connection be forced by the imagination bent to discover or invent some curious inconceivable mythology. And now to the application of the principle that all Vedic terms are *yaugika*, Max Müller translates *reknasas* into gold ornaments, whereas it only means wealth (see *Nighantu*, ii. 10). *Ráti* which signifies the mere act of giving is converted into an 'offering;' *vishvarupa*, which only means one 'having anidea of all forms,' is converted into 'spotted'; *aja* which means 'a man once born in wisdom, *being never born again*,' is converted into a 'goat'; *memyat*, from root *mi* to injure, is given to mean 'bleating'; *suprâng*, which means, from root *prachh* to question, 'one who is able enough to put questions elegantly;' is translated as 'walking onward'; *pathah*, which only means drink or food, is translated into 'path'; and lastly, *indra* and *pushan*, instead of meaning the governing people and the strong are again made to signify two deities with their proper names 'Indra' and 'Púshan.' Concerning the word *patha*, writes Yaska, vi. 7—

पाथोऽन्तरिक्षं । उदकमपि पाथ उच्यते पानात् ।
अन्नमपि पाथ उच्यते पानादेव ॥

Mukhato nayanti, which means, they 'bring out of the organ of speech, or they explain or preach,' is translated by Max Müller into 'they lead before.'

It is thus clear that, in the *one mantra* alone, there are *nine* words that have been wrongly translated by Max Müller, and all is due to this that the *yaugika* sense of the words has been ignored, the *rurhi* or the *laukika* sense being every where forced in the translation. The translation of the *mantra*, according to the sense of the words we have given, will be—

"They who preach that only wealth earned by righteous means should be appropriated and spent, and those born in wisdom, who are well versed in questioning others elegantly, in the science of form, and in correcting the unwise, these and such alone drink the potion of strength and of power to govern."

The connection of this *mantra* with the foregoing is that the *ashwa vidya*, spoken of in the first *mantra*, should be practiced only by those who are possessed of righteous means, are wise, and have the capacity to govern and control.

We come now to the 3rd *mantra* of 162nd Sukta.

एष छागः पुरो अश्वेन वाजिना पूष्णो भागो नीयते विश्वदेव्यः ।
अभिप्रियं यत्पुरोलाशमर्वता त्वष्टेदेनं सौश्रवसाय जिन्वति ॥ ३ ॥

Max Müller translates it thus—

"This goat, destined for all the gods, is led first with the quick horse, as Púshan's share; for Tvashtri himself raises to glory this pleasant offering which is brought with the horse."

Here, again, we find the same artificial stretch of imagination which is the characteristic of this translation. How can the goat be 'destined for all the gods,' and at the same time be 'Púshan's *share*' alone? Here Max Müller gives a reason for the goat being led first as Púshan's share; the reason is that 'Tvashtri himself raises to glory this pleasant offering.' Now who is this Tvashtri, and how is he related to Púshan? How does Tvashtri himself raise to glory this pleasant offering? All these are questions left to be answered by the blank imagination of the reader. Such a translation can only do one service. It is that of making fools of the Vedic *rishis* whom Max Müller supposes to be the authors of the Vedas.

The word *vishwadevyas,* which Max Müller translates as 'destined for all the gods,' can never grammatically mean so. The utmost that one can make for Max Müller on this word is that *vishwadevyas* should mean 'for all the *devas,*' but 'destined' is a pure addition unwarranted by grammar. *Vishwadevya* is formed from *vishwadeva* by the addition of the suffix *yat* in the sense of *tatra sadhu,* (see Ashtadhyayi, IV. 4, 98). The meaning is—

विश्वेषु देवेषु दिव्यगुणेषु साधुर्विश्वदेव्यः

or *Vishwadevyas* is whatsoever is *par excellence* fit to produce useful properties. We have spoken of Max Müller translating *pushan,* which means strength, into a proper noun. *Tvashtri,* which simply means one who befits things, or a skilful hand, is again converted into a proper noun. *Purodasha,* which means food well-cooked, is translated into offering. The words 'which is brought with' are of course Max Müller's addition to put sense into what would otherwise be without any sense. *Arvat,* which, no doubt, sometimes means a horse, here means knowledge. For, if horse were intended, some adjective of significance would have so changed the meaning. *Saushravasaya Jinvati* which means "obtains for purpose of a good food," (*Shravas,* in Vedic Sanskrit, meaning food or *anna*) is translated by Max Müller into 'raises to glory.' The true meaning would be—"The goat possessed of useful properties yields milk as a strengthening food for horses. The best cereal is useful when made into pleasant food well prepared by an apt cook according to the modes dictated by specific knowledge of the properties of foods."

We have criticised Max Müller's translation of the first three *mantras* of this *sukta* in detail, to show how he errs at every step; in every case, the error consisting in taking the *ruhri* meaning instead of the *yaugika* one of the word. It will not be difficult to pass from *mantra* to *mantra* till the hymn is finished, and show that the true origin of all errors lies in not recognising the *yaugika* sense of Vedic terms. But we deem the above three *mantras* as sufficient. We, however, subjoin herewith Max Müller's translation of the remaining *mantras* of this hymn, with our occasional remarks in the foot-notes.

Max Müller's Translation :—

4. When thrice at the proper seasons, men lead around the sacrificial horse which goes to the gods, Púshan's share comes first, the goat, which announces the sacrifice* to the gods.

5. Hotri, Adhvaryu, Avayo, (Pratiprasthatrï), Agnimindha (agnidhra), Gravagrabha (Grasvatut), and the wise Sanstri (Prasastri), may you fill the streams (round the altar) with a sacrifice which is well-prepared and well-acomplished.†

6. They who cut the sacrificial post, and they who carry it, they who make the ring for the post of the horse, and even they who bring together what is cooked for the horse, may their work be with us.

7. He came on—(my prayer has been well performed), the bright backed horse goes to the region of the gods. Wise poets celebrate him, and we have won a good friend for the love of the gods.

8. The halter of the swift one, the heel-ropes of the horse, the head-ropes, the girths, the bridle, and even the grass that has been put into his mouth, may all these which belong to thee be with the gods.

9. What the fly eats of the flesh, what adheres to the stick, or to the axe, or to the hands of the immolator and his nails, may all these which belong to thee be with the gods.‡

---

* The word *yajna* which originally indicates any action requiring association of men or objects, and productive of beneficial results, is always translated by European scholars as sacrifice. The notion of sacrifice is a purely Christian notion, and has no place in Vedic philosophy. It is foreign to the genuine religion of India. Hence all translations in which the word sacrifice occurs are to be rejected as fallacious.

† Max Müller herein puts five words as proper nouns, and therefore does not accept their *yaugika* sense. The words 'round the altar' are supplied by Müller's imagination on the ground that sacrifices are conducted at the altar. Both ideas are foreign to Vedic philosophy.

‡ Here Max Müller does not understand the structure of the sentence. The original words are *ashrasya kravisho* which he takes to mean the flesh of the horse, but *kra visho* is an adjective qualifying *ashvasya*, the whole really means, 'of the pacing horse.' *Kravisho* does not mean 'of the flesh' but 'pacing' from the root *kram*, to pace. The meaning would be, "What the fly eats of whatever dirty adheres to the horse," &c. Again the words *swarau* and *swadhitau* are translated into stick and axe, which is never their meaning.

10. The ordure that runs from the belly, and the smaller particles of raw flesh, may the immolators well prepare all this, and dress the sacrifice till it is well-cooked.*

11. The juice that flows from thy roasted limb on the spit after thou hast been killed, may it not run on the earth, or the grass; may it be given to the gods who desire it.†

12. They who examine the horse when it is roasted, they who say "it smells well, take it away," they who serve the distribution of the meat, may their work also be with us.‡

13. The ladle of the spot where the meat is cooked, and the vessels for sprinkling the juice, the vessels to keep off the heat, the covers of the vessels, the skewers, and the knives, they adorn the horse.

14. Where he walks, where he sits, where he stirs, the foot-fastening of the horse, what he drinks, and what food he eats, may all these which belong to thee, be with the god!

15. May not the fire with smoky smell make thee hiss, may not the glowing cauldron swell and burst. The gods accept the horse if it is offered to them in due form.

16. The cover which they stretch over the horse, and the golden ornaments, the head-ropes of the horse, and the foot-ropes, all these which are dear to the gods, they offer to them.

17. If some one strike these with the heel or the whip that thou mayst lie down, and thou art snorting with all thy might, then I purify all this with my prayer, as with a spoon of clarified butter at the sacrifice.

---

* *Amasya kravisho*, which means 'raw food yet undigested and disposed to come out' is similarly translated by Müller into raw flesh here. *Ama* is the state of the undigested food in the belly. Here again Müller does not follow the structure of the *mantra*.

† *Agnina pachyamanad*, which means 'forced by the heat of anger,' is translated by Müller as roasted; and *hatasya*, which means propelled, is here translated by Müller as "*killed*."

‡ The translation of this mantra is especially noteworthy. The word *wajinam* from *waja*, cereals, is here taken as meaning horse, and Professor Max Müller is so anxious to bring forth the sense of the sacrifice of the horse that, not content with this, he interprets *mansa bhiksham upaste*, which means 'he serves the *absence* of meat' into 'he serves the meat.' Can there be anything more questionable.

18. The axe approaches the 34 ribs of the quick horse, beloved of gods. Do you wisely keep the limbs whole, find out each joint and strike.*

19. One strikes the brilliant horse, two hold it, thus is the custom. These of thy limbs which I have seasonably prepared, I sacrifice in the fire as balls offered to the gods.†

20. May not thy dear soul burn thee, while thou art coming near, may the axe not stick to thy body. May no greedy and unskilful immolator, missing with the sword, throw thy mangled limbs together.

21. Indeed thou diest not thus, thou sufferest not; thou goest to the gods on easy path.

The two horses of Indra, the two deer of the Maruts have been yoked, and the horse come to the shaft of the ass (of the aswins) ‡

22. May this horse give us cattle and horses, men, progeny and all sustaining wealth. May Aditi keep us from sin, may the horse of this sacrifice give us strength."—pp. 553—554.

We leave now Max Müller and his interpretations, and come to another commentator of the Vedas, Sayana. Sayana may truly be called the father of European Vedic scholarship. Sayana is the author from whose voluminous commentaries the Europeans have drunk in the deep wells of mythology. It is upon the interpretation of Madhava Sayana that the translations of Wilson, Benfey and Llanglois are based. It is Sayana whose commentaries are appealed to in all doubtful cases, "If a dwarf on the shoulders of a giant can see further than the giant, he is no less a dwarf in comparison with the giant." If modern exegetes and lexicographers standing at the top of Sayana, *i.e.*, with their main

* The number of ribs mentioned by Müller is worth being counted and verified. *Vankri* which means 'a zigzag motion' is here translated as 'rib.' This requires proof.

† *Twashtu rashvasya* is here translated as 'brilliant horse,' as if *ashva* were the noun and *tvashta* its qualifying adjective. The reverse is the truth. *Twastha* is the noun signifying electricity, and *ashva* is the qualifying adjective signifying all-pervading. The words, "offered to the gods," in the end of the translation are pure addition of Max Müller, to give the whole a mythological coloring.

‡ *Hari* is again as a *rurhi* word translated into two horses of Indra and *prishati* into two deer of *maruts*. The 'Shaft of the ass' is perhaps the greatest curiosity, Max Müller could present, as a sign of mythology.

knowledge of the Vedas borrowed from Sayana, should now exclaim, "Sayana intimates only that sense of the Vedas which was current in India some centuries ago, but comparative philology gives us that meaning which the poets themselves gave to their songs and phrases"; or if they should exclaim that they have the great advantage of putting together ten or twenty passages for examining the sense of a word which occurs in them, which Sayana had not: nothing is to be wondered at. Madhava Sayana, the voluminous commentator of all the Vedas, of the most important Brahmanas and a Kalpa work, the renowned *Mimansist*,—he, the great grammarian, who wrote the learned commentary on Sanskrit radicals: yes, he is still a model of learning and a colossal giant of memory, in comparison to our modern philologists and scholars. Let modern scholars, therefore, always bear in mind, that Sayana is the life of their scholarship, their comparative philology, and their so much boasted interpretation of the Vedas. And if Sayana was himself diseased—whatsoever the value of the efforts of modern scholars—their comparative philology, their new interpretations, and their so-called marvellous achievements cannot but be diseased. Doubt not that the vitality of modern comparative philology and Vedic scholaship is wholly derived from the diseased and defective victuals of Sayana's learning. Sooner or later, the disease will develop its final symptom and sap the foundation of the very vitality it seemed to produce. No branch of a tree can live or flourish when separated from the living stock. No interpretations of the Vedas will, in the end, ever succeed unless they are in accord with the living sense of the Vedas in the Nirukta and the Brahmanas.

I quote here a *mantra* from Rigveda, and will show how Sayana's interpretation radically differs from the exposition of Nirukta. The *mantra* is from Rigveda ix. 96. It runs thus:—

ब्रह्मादेवानां पदवीः कवीनामृषिर्विप्राणां महिषो मृगाणाम् ।
श्येनो गृध्राणां स्वधितिर्वनानां सोमः पवित्र मत्येति रेभन् ॥

Says Sayana :—

"God himself appears as Brahma among the gods, Indra, Agni, &c; He appears as a poet among the dramatists and writers of lyrics; He appears as Vashishtha, &c. among the Brahmanas; He appears as a buffalo among quadrupeds; He appears as an eagle among birds; He appears as an axe in the forest; He appears as the *soma-juice* purified by *mantras* excelling in its power of purification, the sacred waters of the Ganges, &c., &c."

The translation bears the stamp of the time when it was produced. It is the effort of a Pandit to establish his name by appealing to popular prejudice and feeling. Evidently when Sayana wrote, the religion of India was "pantheism" or everything is God; evidently superstition had so far increased that the waters of the Ganges were regarded as sacred; incarnations were believed in; the worship of Brahma, Vasishtha and other *rishis* was at its acme. It was probably the age of the dramatists and poets. Sayana was himself a resident of some city or town. He was not a villager. He was familiar with the axe as an instrument of the destruction of forests, &c., but not with the lightning or fire as a similar but more powerful agent. His translation does not mirror the sense of the Vedas but his own age. His interprepation of *brahma, kavi, deva rishi, vipra, mahisha, mriga, shyena, gridhra, vana soma, pavitra*—of all these words, without one exception, is purely *rurhi* or *laukika*.

Now follows the exposition of Yaska in his Nirukta, xiv, 13. There is not a single word that is not taken in its *yaugika* sense. Says Yaska :—

अथाध्यात्मं ब्रह्मादेवानामित्ययमपि ब्रह्मा भवति देवानां देवनकर्म्मणामिन्द्रियाणां पदवी: कवीनामित्यपि पदं वेत्ति कवीनां कवीयमानानामिन्द्रियाणामृषिर्विप्राणामित्ययमप्यृषिणो भवति विप्राणां व्यापनकर्मणामिन्द्रियाणां महिषो मृगाणामित्ययमपि महान् भवति मार्गणकर्म्मणामिन्द्रियणां श्येनो गृध्रानामितिश्येन आत्मा भवति श्यायते ज्ञान कर्मणो गृध्राणीन्द्रियाणि गृध्यते ज्ञान कर्म्मणो यत एतस्मिंस्तिष्ठति स्वधितिर्वनानामित्ययमपि स्वयं कर्म्माण्यात्मनि धत्ते वनानां वनन कर्मणामिन्द्रियाणां सोम: पवित्रमत्येति सूयमानोऽयमेवैतत सर्वमनुभवत्यात्मगतिमाचष्टे ।

We will now speak of the spiritual sense of the *mantra* as Yaska gives it. It is his object to explain that the human spirit is the central conscious being that enjoys all experience. The external world as revealed by the senses finds its purpose and object and therefore absorption in this central being. The *indriyas* or the senses are called the *devas*, because they have their play in the external phenomenal world, and because it is by them that the external world is revealed to us. Hence *Atma*, the human spirit, is the *brahma devanam*, the conscious entity that presents to its consciousness all that the senses reveal. Similarly, the senses are called the *kavayah*, because one learns by their means. The *Atma*, then, is *padavi kavinam* or the true sentient being that understands the working of the senses. Further, the *Atma* is *rishir vipranam*, the cognizors of sensations; *vipra* meaning the senses as the feelings excited by them pervade the whole body. The senses are also called the *mrigas*, for they hunt about their proper aliment in the external world. *Atma* is *mahisho mriganam*, *i.e.*, the great of all the hunters. The meaning is that it is really through the power of *Atma* that the senses are enabled to find out their proper objects. The *Atma* is called *shyena*, as to it belongs the power of realization; and *gridhras* are the *indriyas*, for they provide the material for such realization. The *Atma*, then, pervades these senses. Further, this *Atma* is *swadhitir vananam*, or the master whom all *indriyas* serve. *Swadhiti* means *Atma*, for the activity of *Atma* is all for itself, man being an end unto himself. The senses are called *vana*, for they serve their master, the human spirit. It is this *Atma* that being pure in its nature enjoys all. Such, then, is the *yaugika* sense which Yaska attaches to the *mantra*. Not only is it all consistent and intelligible unlike Sayana's which conveys no actual sense; not only is each word clearly defined in its *yaugika* meaning, in contradistinction with Sayana who knows no other sense of the word than the popular one; but there is also to be found that simplicity, naturalness and truthfulness of meaning, rendering it independent of all time and space, which, contrasted with the artificiality, burdensomeness and localisation of Sayana's sense, can only proclaim Sayana's complete ignorance of the principles of Vedic interpretation.

It is this Sayana, upon whose commentaries of the Vedas are based the translations of European scholars.

We leave now Max Müller and Sayana with their *rurhi* translations and come to another question, which though remotely connected with the one just mentioned, is yet important enough to be separately treated. It is the question concerning the *Religion of the Vedas.* European scholars and idolatrous superstitious Hindus are of opinion that the Vedas inculcate the worship of innumerable gods and goddesses, *Devatas.* This word, *devata,* is a most fruitful source of error, and it is very necessary that its exact meaning and application should be determined. Not understanding the Vedic sense of this word, *devata* and easily admitting the popular superstitious interpretation of a belief in mythological gods and goddesses, crumbling into wretched idolatry, European scholars have imagined the Vedas to be full of the worship of such materials, and have gone so far in their reverence for the Vedas as to degrade its religion even below polytheism and perhaps at par with atheism. In their fit of benevolence, the European scholars have been gracious enough to endow this religion with a title, a name, and that is Henotheism.

After classifying religions into polytheistic, dualistic and monotheistic, remarks Max Müller, "It would certainly be necessary to add two other classes—the *henotheistic* and the *atheistic.* Henotheistic religions differ from polytheistic, because, although they recognize the existence of various deities, or names of deities, they represent each deity as independent of all the rest, as the only deity present in the mind of the worshipper at the time of his worship and prayer. *This character is very prominent in the religion of the Vedic poets.* Although many gods are invoked in different hymns, sometimes also in the same hymn, yet there is no rule of precedence established among them; and, according to the varying aspects of nature, and the varying cravings of human heart, it is sometimes Indra, the god of the blue sky, sometimes Agni, the god of fire, sometimes Varuna, the ancient god of the firmament, who are praised as supreme without any suspicion of rivalry, or any idea of subordination. This peculiar phase of religion, this worship of single gods forms probably everywhere the first stage in the growth of polytheism, and deserves therefore a separate name."*

To further illustrate the principles of this new religion, henotheism, says Max Müller, "When these individual gods are invoked, they are not conceived as limited by the power of others as superior or inferior in rank. Each god is to the mind of the supplicant as good as all the gods. He is felt, at the time, as a real divinity, as supreme and absolute, in spite of the necessary limitation which, to our mind, a plurality of gods must entail on every single god. All the rest disappear for a moment from the vision of the poet, and he only who is to fulfil their desires stands in full light before the eyes of the worshippers. 'Among you, O gods, there is none that is small, none that is young; you are all great indeed,' is a sentiment which, though perhaps, not so distinctly expressed as by Manu Vaivasvata, nevertheless, underlies all the poetry of the Veda. Although the gods are sometimes distinctly invoked as the great and the small, the young and the old (Rv. i, 27-13), this is only an attempt to find out the most comprehensive expression for the divine powers, and nowhere is any of the gods represented as the slave of others."

As an illustration, "when Agni, the lord of fire, is addressed by the poet, he is spoken of as the first god, not inferior even to Indra. While Agni is invoked, Indra is forgotten; there is no competition between the two, nor any rivalry between them and other gods. This is a most important feature in the religion of the Veda, and has never been taken into consideration by those who have written on the history of ancient polytheism."†

* Max Müller: Lectures on the Science of Religion, London, 1873, pp. 141-142.

† Max Müller: History of Ancient Sanskrit Literature, pp. 552-553.

We have seen what Max Müller's view of the Religion of the Vedas is. We may be sure that the review of other European scholars also cannot be otherwise. Is henotheism really, then, the religion of the Vedas? Is the worship of *devatas* an essential feature of Vedic worship? Are we to believe Max Müller, and assert that the nation to which he hesitates to deny instinctive monotheism has so far uprooted its instincts as to fall down to an acquired belief in henotheism? * No, not so. Vedas, the sacred books of the primitive Aryans, are the purest record of the highest form of monotheism possible to conceive. Scholars cannot long continue to misconstrue the Vedas, and ignore the laws of their interpretation. Says Yaska:—

अथातो दैवतं तद्यानिनामानि प्रधान्यस्तुतीनां देवतानां तद्दैवतमित्याचक्षते सैषा देवतोपपरीक्षा यत्काम ऋषिर्यस्यां देवतायामर्थपत्यमिच्छन् स्तुतिं प्रयुङ्क्ते तद्दैवतः स मन्त्रो भवति ॥—Nirukta, vii, 1.

Devata is a general term applied to those substances whose attributes are explained in a *mantra*. The sense of the above is that when it is known which substance it is that forms the subject of exposition in the *mantra*, the term signifying that substance is called the *devata* of the *mantra*. Take, for instance, the *mantra*,

अग्निं दूतं पुरोदधे हव्यवाहमुपब्रुवे ॥ देवां ॥ २ ॥ आसादयादिह ॥ यजु: २२ । १७ ॥

"I present to your consideration *agni* which is the fruitful source of worldly enjoyments, which is capable of working as though it were a messenger, and is endowed with the property of preparing all our foods. Hear ye, and do the same."

Since it is *agni* that forms the subject-matter of this *mantra*, *agni* would be called the *devata* of this *mantra*. Hence, says Yaska, a *mantra* is of that *devata*, with the object of expressing *whose* properties, God, the Omniscient, revealed the *mantra*.

We find an analogous sense of the word *devata* in another part of Nirukta. Says Yaska—

---

* Max Müller: History of Ancient Sanskrit Literature, p. 546.

कर्म्म सम्पत्तिर्मन्त्रो वेदे ॥ Nirukta, i. 2.

'Whenever the process of an art is described. 'the *mantra* that completely describes that process is called the *devata* (or the index) of that process.'

It is in this sense that the *devata* of a *mantra* is the index, the essential key-note of the meaning of the *mantra*. There is in this analysis of the word no reference to any gods or goddesses, no mythology, no element worship, no henotheism. If this plain and simple meaning of *devata* were understood, no more will the *mantras*, having *marut* for their *devata* or *agni* for their *devata*, be regarded as hymns addressed to the storm-god or the god of fire; but it will be perceived that these *mantras* treat respectively of the properties of *marut* and of the properties of fire. It will then be regarded, as said elsewhere in Nirukta—

देवो दानाद्वा दीपनाद्वा द्योतनाद्वा द्यु स्थानो भवतीति वा ॥

Nirukta, vii. 15.

that whatsoever or whosoever is capable of conferring some advantage upon us, capable of illuminating things, or capable of explaining them to us, and lastly, the Light of all lights, these are the fit objects to be called *devatas*. This is not in any way inconsistent with what has gone before. For, the *devata* of a *mantra*, being the key-note of the sense of the *mantra*, is a word capable of rendering an *explanation* of the *mantra*, and hence is called the *devata* of that *mantra*. Speaking of these *devatas*, Yaska writes something which even goes to show that people of his time had not even the slightest notion of the gods and goddesses of Max Müller and superstitious Hindus—gods, and goddesses that are now *forced* upon us under the Vedic designation, *devata*. Says he—

अस्ति ह्याचारोबहुलम् लोके देवदेवत्यमतिथिदेवत्यं पितृदेवतं ॥

Nirukta, vii. 4.

'We often find in common practice of the world at large, that learned men, parents, and *atithis*, (or those guest-missionaries who have no fixed residence, but wander about from place to place benefiting the world by their religious instructions), are regarded as *devatas* or called by the names of *devatas.*' It is clear from the above quotation, that religious teachers, parents and learned men, these alone, or the like, were called *devatas* and no others, in Yaska's time. Had Yaska known of any such idolatry or henotheism or *devata* worship which superstitious Hindus are so fond of, and which Professor Max Müller is so intent to find in the Vedas, or had any such worship prevailed in his time, even though he himself did not share in this worship, it is impossible that he should not have made any mention of it at all, especially when speaking of the common practice among men in general. There can be no doubt that element worship, or nature worship, is not only foreign to the Vedas and the ages of Yaska and Panini and Vedic *rishis* and *munis*, but that idolatry and its parent mythology, at least in so far as Aryavarta is concerned, are the products of recent times.

To return to the subject. We have seen that Yaska regards the names of those substances whose properties are treated of in the *mantra* as the *devatas*. What substances, then, are the *devatas?* They are all that can form the subject of human knowledge. All human knowledge is limited by two conditions, *i.e., time* and *space*. Our knowledge of causation is mainly that of succession of events. And succession is nothing but an *order* in *time*. Secondly, our knowledge must be a knowledge of something and that something must be somewhere. It must have a *locality* of its existence and occurrence. Thus far, the *circumstances* of our knowledge, *time* and *locality*. Now to the essentials of knowledge. The most exhaustive division of human knowledge is between objective and subjective. Objective knowledge is the knowledge of all that passes without the human body. It is the knowledge of the phenomena of the external universe. Scientific men have arrived at the conclusion that natural philosophy, *i.e.*, philosophy of the material universe, reveals the presence of two things, matter and force. Matter as matter is not known to us. It is only the play of forces in matter producing effects, sensible, that is known to us. Hence the knowledge of external world is resolved into the knowledge of *force* with its modifications. We come next to subjective knowledge. In speaking of subjective knowledge, there is firstly the ego, the *human spirit*, the conscious entity; secondly, the internal phenomena of which the human spirit is conscious. The internal phenomena are of two kinds. They are either the voluntary, intelligent, self-conscious activities of the mind, which may hence be designated *deliberate activities*, or the passive modifications effected in the functions of the body by the presence of the human spirit. These may therefore be called the *vital activities*.

An *apriori* analysis, therefore, of the knowable leads us to six things, *time, locality, force, human spirit, deliberate activities,* and *vital activities*. These things, then, are fit to be called *devatas*. The conclusion to be derived from the above enumeration is, that, if the account of *Nirukta* concerning Vedic *devatas*, as we have given, be really true, we should find Vedas inculcating these six things—*time, locality, force, human spirit, deliberate activities* and *vital activities*, as *devatas* and no others. Let us apply the crucial test.

We find, however, the mention of 33 *devatas* in such *mantras* as these:—

II. यस्य त्रयस्त्रिंशद्देवा अङ्गे गात्रा विभेजिरे ।

तान्वै त्रयस्त्रिंशद्देवानेके ब्रह्मविदो विदुः ॥ अथर्व X. xxii. 4-27.

1. त्रयस्त्रिंशतास्तुवतभूतान्यशाम्यन् प्रजापतिः परमेष्ठ्याधिपतिरासीत् ।

Yajur, xiv. 31.

"The Lord of all, the Ruler of the universe, the Sustainer of all, holds all things by 33 *devatas*."

"The knowers of true theology recognize the 33 *devatas* performing their proper organic functions, as existing in and by Him, the One and Only."

Let us, therefore, see what these 33 *davatas* are, so that we may be able to compare them with our *apriori* deductions and settle the question. We read in Shatapatha Brahmana—

सहोवाच महिमान एवैषामेते त्रयस्त्रिं शत्वेव देवा इति। कतमेते त्रयस्त्रिं शदि त्यष्टौ वसव एकादशरुद्रा द्वादशादित्यास्ता एकत्रिंशदिन्द्रश्चैव प्रजापतिश्च त्रयस्त्रिं शाविति ॥३॥ कतमे वसव इति। अग्निश्च पृथवीच वायुश्चान्तरिक्षं चादित्यश्च द्यौश्च चन्द्रमाश्च नक्षत्राणि चैते वसव एतेषु हीदं सर्वं वसुहितमेते हीदꣳ सर्वं वासयन्ते तद्यदिदम् सर्वं वासयन्ते तस्माद्वसव इति ॥ ४ ॥ कतमे रुद्रा इति। दशेमे पुरुषे प्राणा आत्मैकादशस्ते यदास्मान्मर्त्याच्छरीरादुत्क्रामन्त्यथ रोदयन्ति तद्यद्रोदयन्ति तस्माद्रुद्रा इति ॥ ५ ॥ कतम आदित्या इति। द्वादश मासाः संवत्सरस्यैता आदित्या एते हीदꣳ सर्वमाददाना यन्ति तद्यदिदꣳ सर्वमाददाना यन्ति तस्मादादित्य इति ॥ ६ ॥ कतम इन्द्रः कतमः प्रजापतिरिति। स्तनयित्नुरेवेन्द्रो यज्ञः प्रजापतिरिति। कतमः स्तनयित्नुरित्यशनिरिति कतमो यज्ञ इति पशव इति ॥ ७ ॥ कतमेते त्रयो देवा इतीम एव त्रयोलोका एषु हीमे सर्वे देवा इति। कतमौ द्वौ देवावित्यन्नं चैव प्राणश्चेति। कतमो अध्यर्ध इति योऽयं पवते ॥ ८ ॥ तदाहुः यदयमेक एव पवतेऽथ कथमध्यर्ध इति यदस्मिन्नदꣳसर्वमध्यार्ध्नोत्तेनाध्यर्ध इति। कतम एको देव इति सब्रह्म, त्यदित्याचक्षत ॥ xiv. 16.*

The meaning of the above is :—

"Says Yajnavalkya, O Shâkalya, there are 33 *devatas*; 8 *vasus* 11 *rudras*, 12 *âdityás*, *indra* and *prâjâpati*; 33 on the whole. The eight *vasus* are 1. heated cosmic bodies, 2. planets, 3. atmospheres, 4. superterrestrial spaces, 5. suns, 6. rays of ethereal space, 7. satellites, 8. stars. These are called *vasus* (abodes), for the whole group of existences resides in them, for they are the abode of all that lives, moves, or exists. The eleven *rudras* are the ten nervauric forces enlivening the human frame, and the eleventh is the human spirit. These are called the *rudras* (from root *rud* to weep), because when they desert the body, it becomes dead, and the relations of the dead, in consequence of

* *Vide* Swami Dayanand Saraswati's Veda Bhashya Bhumika, p. 66.

this desertion, begin to *weep*. The twelve *âdityâs* are the twelve solar months, marking the course of time. They are called *âdityâs* as by their cyclic motion they produce changes in all objects, and hence the *lapse of the term of existence for each object*. *Adityâs* means that which causes such a lapse. *Indra* is the all-pervading *electricity* or *force*. *Prajâpati* is *yajna* (or an active voluntary association of objects, on the part of man, for the purposes of art, or association with other men for purposes of teaching or learning). It also means the *useful animals*. *Yajna* and useful animals are called *prajâpati*, as it is by such actions and by such animals that the world at large derives its materials of sustenance. "What, then, are the three *devatas?*"—Asks Shâkalya. Says Yâjnavalkya, they are *locality, name* and *birth*. 'What are the two *devatas?*'—asked he. Yâjnavalky, replied, 'the positive substances, *prána*, and negative substances, *anna*. *Adhyardha* is the universal electricity, the sustainer of the universe known as *sûtrâtmâ*. Lastly, he inquired, 'Who is the one *Devata?*' And Yâjnavalkya replied, "God, the adorable."

These, then, are the thirty-three *devatas* mentioned in the Vedas. Let us see how far this analysis agrees with our *a priori* deduction. The eight *vasus* enumerated in Shatpatha Brahmana are clearly the *localities*; the twelve *âdityâs* comprise *time;* the eleven *rudras* include, firstly, the *ego*, the *human spirit*, and secondly, the ten *nervauric forces* which may be approximately taken for the *vital activities* of the mind, *electricity* is the all-pervading *force*; whereas *prajâpati, yajna or pashus* may be roughly regarded as comprising the objects of intelligent *deliberate activities* of the mind.

When thus understood, the 33 *devatas* will correspond with the six elements of our rough analysis. Since the object, here, is not so much to show exactness of detail as general coincidence, partial differences may be left out of account.

It is clear, then, that the interpretation of *devatas* which Yaska gives is the only interpretation that is consistent with the Vedas and the Brahmanas. That no doubt may be left concerning the pure monotheistic worship of the ancient Aryas, we quote from Nirukta again—

माहाभाग्याद्देवताया एक आत्मा बहुधा स्तूयते एकस्यात्मनोऽन्ये देवाः प्रत्यङ्गानि भवन्ति। कर्मजन्मान आत्मजन्मान आत्मैवैषां रथो भवति आत्माऽश्वा आत्मायुधमात्मेष वा आत्मा सर्वं देवस्य देवस्य॥ Nirukta vii. 4.

"Leaving off all other *devatas*, it is only the Supreme Soul that is worshipped on account of its omnipotence. Other *devatas* are but the *pratyangas* of this Supernal Soul, *i.e.*, they but *partially* manifest the glory of God. All these *devatas* owe their birth and power to Him. In Him they have their play. Through Him they exercise their beneficial influences by attracting properties useful and repelling properties injurious. He alone is the All in All of all the *devatas*."

From the above it will be clear that, in so far as worship is concerned, the ancient Aryas adored the Supreme Soul only, regarding Him as the life, the sustenance and dormitory of the world. And yet pious Christian missionaries and more pious Christian philologists are never tired of propagating the lie before the world that the Vedas inculcate the worship of many gods and goddesses. Writes a Christian missionary in India :—

"*Monotheism* is a belief in the existence of one God only ; *polytheism* is a belief in the plurality of gods. Max Müller says, 'If we must employ technical terms, the religion of the Veda is polytheism, not monotheism.' The 27th hymn of the 1st Ashtaka of the Rigveda concludes as follows : 'Veneration to the great gods, veneration to the lesser, veneration to the young, veneration to the old ; we worship the gods as well as we are able : may I not omit the praise of the older divinities." *

The pious Christian thus ends his remarks on the religion of the Vedas. "Pantheism and polytheism are often combined, but mono-

---

* John Murdoch : Religious Reform, Part III, Vedic Hinduism.

theism, in the strict sense of the word, is not found in Hinduism.' Again says the pious missionary, "Ram Mohan Roy, as already mentioned, despised the hymns of the Vedas, he spoke of the Upanishads as the Vedas, and thought that they taught monotheism. The Chhandogya formula, '*ekamevadwitiyam brahma*,' was also adopted by Keshub Chander Sen. But it does not mean that there is no second God, but that there is no second anything—a totally different doctrine." Thus it is obvious that Christians, well saturated with the truth of God, are not only anxious to see monotheism off the Vedas, but even off the Upanishats. Well might they regard their position as safe, beyond assail, on the strength of such translations as these:—

"In the beginning there arose the Hiranyagarbha (*the golden germ*) —He was the one born lord of all this. He established the earth and this sky:—Who is the God to whom we shall offer our sacrifice?"—*Max Müller.*

"He who gives breath, He who gives strength, whose command all the bright gods revere, whose shadow is immortality, whose shadow is death:—Who is the God to whom we shall offer our sacrifice?"—*Ibid.*

Hiranyagarbha, which means 'God in whom the whole luminous universe resides in a potential state' is translated into the *golden germ*. The word *jatah* is detached from its proper construction and placed in apposition with *patir*, thus giving the sense of "the one born lord of all this." Perhaps, there is a deeper meaning in this Christian translation. Some day, not in the very remote future, these Christians will discover that the *golden germ* means '*conceived by the Holy Ghost*,' whereas 'the one born lord of all' alludes to Jesus Christ. In one of those future happy days, this *mantra* of the Veda will be quoted as an emblematic of a prophecy, in the dark distant past, of the advent of a Christ whom the ancients knew not. How could they, then, adore him, but in the language of mystic interrogation? Hence the translation, "Who is the God to whom we shall offer our sacrifice?" Even the second *mantra*, Max Müller's translation of which we have subjoined above, has been differently translated by an audacious Christian. What Max Müller translates as "He who gives breath," was translated by this believer in the word of God, as "He who sacrificed Himself, *i.e.*, *Jesus Christ.*" The original words in Sanskrit are 'य आत्मदा,' which mean "he who gives spiritual knowledge."

Let us pass from these *mantras* and the misinterpretations of Christians to clear proofs of monotheism in the Vedas. We find in Rigveda the very *mantra* which yields the *golden germ* to European interpreters. It runs thus—

हिरण्यगर्भः समवर्त्तताग्रे भूतस्य जातः पतिरेक आसीत्।
स दाधार पृथिवीं द्यामुतेमां कस्मै देवाय हविषा विधेम॥

"God existed in the beginning of creation, the only Lord of the unborn universe. He is the Eternal Bliss whom we should praise and adore."

In Yajur Veda, xvii. 19, we find—

विश्वतश्चक्षुरुत विश्वतो मुखो विश्वतो बाहुरुत विश्वतस्पात्।
संबाहुभ्यांधमति सं पतत्रैर्द्यावाभूमी जनयन् देव एकः॥

"Being all vision, all power, all motion in Himself, He sustains with His power the whole universe. Himself being One alone."

And in Atharva Veda, XIII. iv. 16—21, we find—

न द्वितीयो न तृतीयश्चतुर्थो नाप्युच्यते ....
स एष एक एक वृदेक एव। सर्वे अस्मिन् देवा एकवृतो भवन्ति॥

"There are neither two gods, nor three, nor four,.........nor ten. He is one and only one and pervades the whole universe. All other things live, move and have their existence in Him."